Bathtubs
Slides
Roller Coaster
Rails

Bathtubs

Slides

Roller Coaster Rails

SIMPLE MACHINES
THAT ARE REALLY
INCLINED PLANES

BY CHRISTOPHER LAMPTON
PICTURES BY CAROL NICKLAUS

THE MILLBROOK PRESS · BROOKFIELD, CT
A GATEWAY BOOK

Cataloging-in-Publication Data

Lampton, Christopher
Bathtubs, slides and roller coaster rails /
Christopher Lampton; pictures by Carol Nicklaus
Brookfield, CT., Millbrook Press, 1991.
32 p. : ill.
Includes glossary and index.
ISBN: 1-878841-44-0 (pbk.)
1. Simple Machines. 2. Inclined planes.
3. Science - Experiments. I. Title. II. Carol Nicklaus, ill.

123456789-WO-96 95 94 93 92

Bathtubs
Slides
Roller Coaster Rails

Do you want to feel big and strong in a hurry? Just use a machine.

Machines can't really make you bigger or stronger than you are. But they can help you do many things you might find hard or impossible without them.

A car can carry us much farther than we could easily walk. An airplane can take us even farther and faster than a car. An elevator can lift us higher than we could comfortably climb. Cars, airplanes, and elevators are examples of **complex machines.**

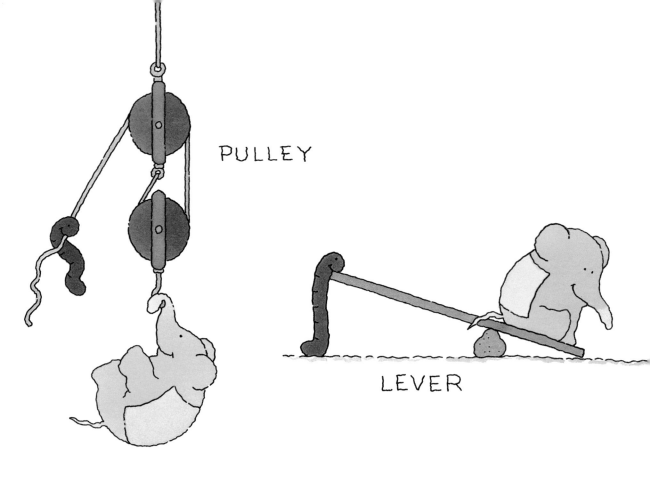

PULLEY

LEVER

Complex machines are made up of many small parts that work together. **Simple machines** do not have many parts. They help us do things but they don't do all the work for us. Lots of things we use every day, such as wheels and axles, pulleys, and levers, are simple machines. But the simple machine we're going to look at here is called the inclined plane.

An inclined plane is really nothing more than a slanted surface, like a ramp. In fact, a ramp is an inclined plane. A ramp is a machine because it helps you perform work that might be difficult or impossible otherwise.

WHEEL
AND
AXLE

INCLINED PLANE

Let's pretend that you're a teenager and have a number of jobs mowing lawns for the summer. You have a big power mower and the use of your parents' truck to move the mower from place to place. Sounds like a great setup, right? Except, if you can't lift the mower, how are you going to get it onto the truck?

Yes, you could hire an assistant, but that would cost money. Better yet, an inclined plane could solve your problem. If you were to prop a wide board against the back of the truck, you could push your mower up the ramp and onto the truck. You would have to use some muscle power, but you could raise the mower from the ground to the truck by yourself.

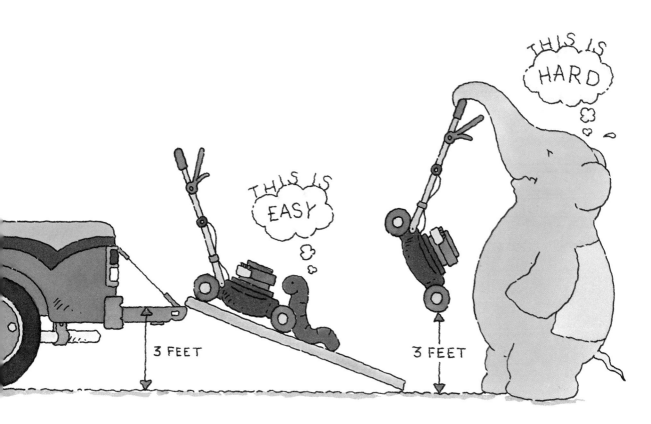

Remember that we said machines allow you to perform tasks that would be hard or impossible without them. So, even though a ramp doesn't look like a machine, you just saw how it could help you raise the lawn mower that you couldn't lift alone.

The machine known as the inclined plane allowed you to use less effort than you needed to lift the lawn mower straight off the ground. How was this possible? Let's build our own ramp and see.

Fill a box that is about 1 foot high with books or some other heavy objects so that the box won't move. Prop a 4-foot-long board up against the box. You have now built an inclined plane. You see why it's called simple!

HEAVY BOOKS

4-FOOT-LONG BOARD

1 FOOT HIGH

Find a toy truck that's heavy enough so that you can feel its weight when you hold it in your hand. Lift the truck 1 foot off the floor. The heavier it is, the more force you'll have to use to lift it.

Gravity is the force that pulls things down to earth. The **weight** of the truck is the force of gravity pulling the truck down to earth. The force that you need to lift the truck is the force that you need to overcome gravity.

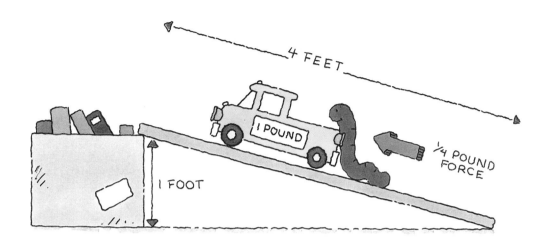

Push the truck from the bottom of the ramp to the top of the box (which is 1 foot high). You'll find that you used less force to push your truck to the top of the ramp than you used lifting it straight up the same distance.

In this experiment, you had to push the truck farther to raise it 1 foot than when you lifted it straight up. But pushing it was easier than lifting it, wasn't it? So you made a trade-off. You chose to push the truck the longer distance because you wanted to use less force.

A toy truck isn't very heavy; you can probably lift yours straight up without using much force. You didn't really need a ramp, so the trade-off might not seem important.

But remember the lawn mower. Let's say the back of the truck is 3 feet off the ground. In that situation you really need the help of the inclined plane. Your muscles can't provide the force required to lift the weight of a 100-pound lawn mower straight up 3 feet. But whether you are pushing the mower up the ramp or raising the lawn mower 3 feet onto the truck, you are still performing the work of lifting the mower up 3 feet. So why does it take less effort to push the mower up the ramp?

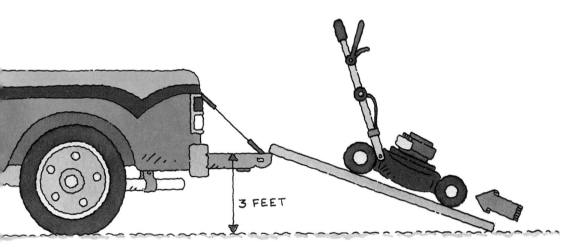

3 FEET

1 POUND × 1 FOOT = WORK

¼ POUND × 4 FEET = SAME AMOUNT OF WORK

FORCE × DISTANCE = WORK

To answer this question, we need to look at how scientists define work. They measure how much force (F) you use to move something and the distance (D) you move to do it. By multiplying these two numbers, scientists arrive at a definition of how much work is done. In other words, Force × Distance = Work.

So, let's say that your truck weighed 1 pound. When you raised the truck straight up, you moved it a distance of 1 foot and used a force of 1 pound. When you pushed the truck up the ramp, you pushed it a distance of 4 feet but you needed a force of only one fourth of a pound. In either case you performed the same amount of work.

When a machine allows you to change the amount of force you use to accomplish a task, we say that you have gained a **mechanical advantage.**

Here's an experiment that will show you mechanical advantage in action:

You'll need a thin rubber band and a piece of string. Tie one end of the string to the truck and the other end to the rubber band. Lift the truck straight up from the floor with the rubber band. Notice how far the rubber band stretches.

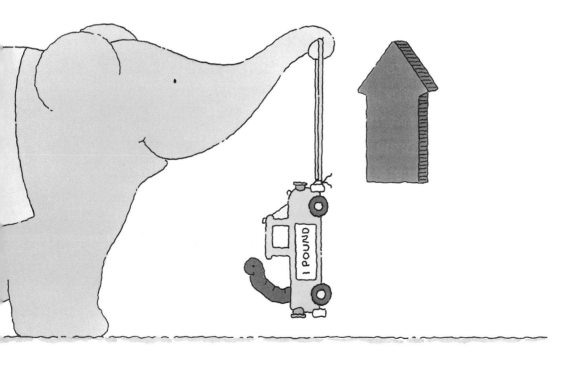

Now use the rubber band to pull the truck slowly and smoothly up the ramp. Again, notice how far the rubber band stretches.

The rubber band shows you how much force you are using. The less it stretches, the less force you are using. The more it stretches, the more force you are using. The rubber band stretched less when you pulled the truck up the ramp than when you lifted it straight up into the air, didn't it? So, the ramp let you use less force or, in other words, you gained a mechanical advantage.

The amount of force needed to move an object up an inclined plane depends on the slant of the plane. To raise an object to a certain height, the longer the ramp is, the flatter its slant, The shorter the ramp is, the steeper its slant. On a long gentle ramp it takes very little force to move an object upward. On a short steep ramp it takes almost as much force as it would take to lift an object straight up.

Use the rubber band and truck to see how this works. Tilt the ramp at different angles. Notice how much the rubber band stretches at each angle. You'll see that the steeper the angle, the greater the stretch. And, of course, the greater the stretch, the more force you are using to move the truck.

The trick in using an inclined plane is to find the right trade-off. The best inclined plane lets you use it with a comfortable amount of force—without taking all day to get to the top of the ramp!

You don't have to use much force at all to move something down an inclined plane. The force called gravity pulls it down for you, just as it pulls you back to earth when you jump off the ground.

If you put your truck at the top of the ramp that you made, it would roll right down to the floor by itself. That's a better way to return the truck to the floor than by dropping it from a foot in the air. Just as ramps can help us lift things, they can help us lower things safely without breaking them.

But what would happen if you put a book or a block or another flat object at the top of the ramp? It would not slide down like the truck did. That's because the truck rolls on wheels, while the book's surface presses directly against the surface of the ramp. The force that resists the movement of the book is **friction.**

The heavier or rougher the object you're trying to slide down the ramp, the greater the friction. The surface of the ramp can increase the friction too. The rougher the surface of the board you are using for a ramp, the more friction there will be.

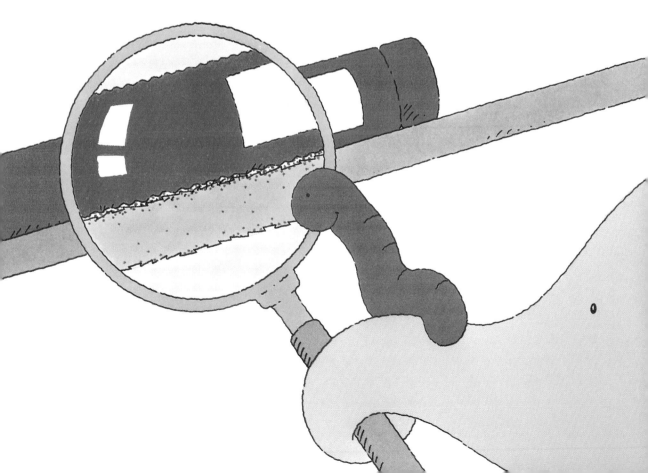

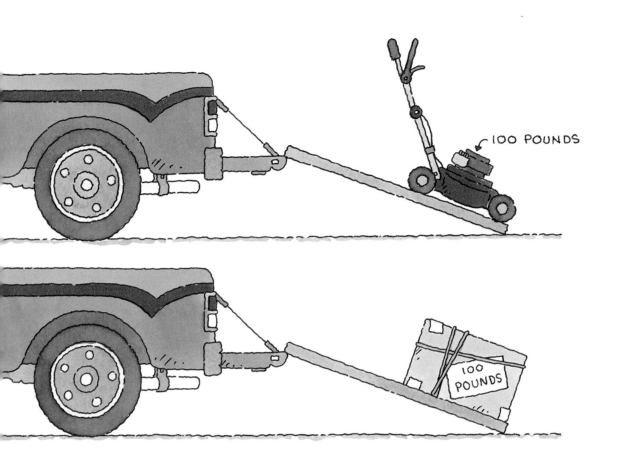

100 POUNDS

100 POUNDS

Which do you think would require less force to push up the ramp to the truck: a lawn mower, or a large box of the same weight as the lawn mower?

Have you ever watched a friend have a great ride down a slide—and then come down yourself, bumping and stopping all the way? Can you figure out why this might happen? Could it have anything to do with what you were wearing?

Now that you know all about inclined planes, keep your eyes open. You'll see them all around you.

For instance, the next time you take a bath, notice what happens to the water when you open the drain. The bottom of the tub is an ever-so-slightly angled inclined plane with a drain at the bottom. The force of gravity moves the water down the inclined plane to the drain.

In winter you can have a great time on an inclined plane. Whether you're on skis or a sled, you can speed down snowy hills. When the ground is covered with snow, there is little friction to slow you down.

When the weather is warmer, you can find inclined planes in amusement parks. Water slides carry you in a torrent of water from the top of a tower down to a pool.

Have you ever taken a ride on a roller coaster? Complex machines pull the cars to the top of a steep hill. Then gravity pulls them down an inclined plane on the other side for a wild and rapid ride.

After a ride like that, you might be thirsty. At the soft-drink machine, notice how the bottle or can slides down an inclined plane into the dispenser slot.

A mountain road doesn't go straight up the side of a mountain. It would be too steep for a car to climb.

You might imagine building an inclined plane to lessen the steepness of the grade. But even if the mountain were only 1 mile high, the inclined plane would have to cover such a huge distance that you'd have to start it miles away! And you'd have to build it on tall supports to hold it in the air.

Instead, a mountain road is often a series of inclined planes that zigzags up the mountainside—or spirals around the whole mountain, like the threads on a screw. And it's cut out of the mountain itself so that it doesn't need tall supports.

A screw is a special type of inclined plane. If you look carefully at a screw, you will see that it is really an inclined plane that goes around a shaft, just the way a mountain road wraps around a mountain.

A wedge is another special type of inclined plane that we can use to raise things up or split things apart. The blade of a knife is a wedge. Can you think of other types of wedges?

Inclined planes may be simple, but they're among the most useful machines around.

And that's the plane truth!

Index / Glossary

Complex machine: a machine made up of combinations of simple machines, 7–8.

Force: the effort applied to move something, 17.

Friction: the force that resists the movement of two objects touching each other, 23.

Gravity: the force that pulls things down to earth, 14.

Inclined plane: a slanted surface, 8–9.

Mechanical advantage: the relationship between the effort you put into a machine and the force you get out of it, 18–19.

Simple machine: a device that allows us to reduce the amount of effort we use to do work, 8.

Trade-off: the exchange between distance and force that occurs when we do work, 15–16.

Weight: the force of gravity pulling something down to earth, 14.

Work: force times distance equals work, 17.